# Spiritual Centers in Man

by Manly P. Hall

**SPIRITUAL CENTERS IN MAN**



**ISBN 0-89314-383-9**

*(Formerly published under the title of* "AN ESSAY ON THE FUNDAMENTAL PRINCIPLES OF OPERATIVE OCCULTISM"*)*

---

*Published by*

THE PHILOSOPHICAL RESEARCH SOCIETY
3910 Los Feliz Boulevard
Los Angeles, CA 90027 USA

*Telephone* 323.663.2167
*Fax* 323.663.9443
*Website* www.prs.org
*E-mail* info@prs.org

*Printed in the United States of America*

## Preface

We regard growth as a natural process but the phenomenon of unfoldment is actually a revelation of the release of the spiritual potential with which all creatures have been endowed. Evolution is actually a kind of ideation or an expansion of consciousness through bodies. Jacob Boehme, the German mystic, describes the soul as a tree with its roots in the heart and its branches extending through all the regions of space. The fruit of this tree is for the healing of the nations, and the shade which it provides is consolation and protection for those who are weary of worldliness.

The sacred institutions of both Eastern and Western nations have taught the science of human regeneration. They have revealed the paths that lead to liberation from mental, emotional, and physical suffering. In this essay I have attempted to show that growth is a pleasant journey and that those who keep the laws of living place themselves in the keeping of these laws. Some follow along a devotional path; others are led to peace through philosophy; and still others by a scientific kind of alchemy involving a transmutation of character. The victory of the soul over circumstances through physiological changes is discussed in the pages that follow.

*Manly P. Hall*
*Los Angeles, California*

### The Opening of the Third Eye

This painting of the head of Minerva shows, in part, the activities of the pineal gland and the pituitary body at the time of the phenomenon commonly termed "the opening of the Third Eye." The Kundalini fire is seen rising upward through the spinal canal into the pons of the medulla oblongata. The golden light radiating from the base of the brain, at the back, gradually increases in size and intensity until it forms the nimbus, or halo, of the saint. The pituitary body is here shown surrounded by an elliptic rose aura. The pineal gland—the Third Eye of the Mysteries—is here depicted as blue in color and surround by a radiating blue spectrum, but blue decidedly predominates. The tiny vibrating finger on the pineal gland points directly toward the pituitary body. This finger, vibrating at a very high rate of speed, is the actual cause of true spiritual illumination.

## SPIRITUAL CENTERS IN MAN

The question is asked, "What must I do to unfold the divine powers latent within myself?" While it is not possible to give a direct answer to this question, we may cast some light on the subject by defining the fundamental principles upon which the Mystery schools of all ages were established as institutions of philosophic, ethical, and religious culture. The Schools of the Mysteries are composed of illumined men and women who have been accepted into the company of the Immortals.

To reach this exalted position requires an almost inconceivable amount of preparatory labor; for if man would associate with these advanced types of humanity, he must raise himself to their level. Realizing that nothing is more dangerous than the indiscriminate circulation of occult secrets, the Mysteries established their schools for the purpose of concealing rather than revealing knowledge. They were the original and sole custodians of all the divine arts and sciences, the secret keys to which they revealed only to those whom they considered qualified to receive them. Inasmuch as man's power increases with his knowledge, the secrets of Nature's finer forces cannot be revealed to him until he has passed through these Mysteries, which test him as to his motive and demand certain standards of moral and philosophic excellence.

Before the candidate is in a position to begin his studies in occult philosophy (which, if successfully completed, will result in discipleship and final admission into the Mysteries) he must first lay the groundwork by familiarizing himself with certain systems of ethics, and gain at least reasonable proficiency in several material arts and sciences.

*(1) The candidate must realize the value of education.* While the ignorant person may be capable of spiritual growth, the fact remains that man's ethical progress is seriously retarded through ignorance of the material arts and sciences. Not realizing the great value of discipline, many students of the occult sciences ridicule modern educational systems, which excel because they discipline the mind. Learning how to study is a prerequisite to effective studying. Before it is possible to think, it is necessary to train the mind in reason, continuity, and logic—the essentials of thought.

In the last analysis, all the so-called material arts and sciences are reflections of the Secret Wisdom. A man with an understanding of mathematics cannot help but know more of the Divine Plan than one without. Pythagoras demanded proficiency in music, mathematics, and astronomy of all candidates seeking admission into his school.

Before a candidate can honestly seek admission to the Temple of Wisdom, he must prepare his offerings and bring them to the Temple. The only possible offering which he can make is himself, and this offering is acceptable only when it is usable for the dissemination of wisdom. The more nearly perfect that vehicle is, the greater its usefulness. If able to speak a dozen languages, he has a decided asset. If skilled in chemistry, gifted in oratory, clear in thought, he has valuable talents which can be quickly turned to the service of mankind. If the candidate, regardless of his sincerity, presents himself at the door of the Temple ignorant and untrained, it is first necessary to equip him for his work. This preparatory training requires years. A person willing to consecrate himself unselfishly to the service of God—the first requisite for entrance into the Temple—should certainly be willing first to educate himself by learning what the material world has to teach. He must never seek for the Masters of Wisdom until he has something of real value to offer them, for usefulness is to a great measure limited by intelligence.

(2) *The candidate must understand the importance of continuity.* The curse of the modern world is its inability to finish the enterprises which it begins. As a child starts several things but completes none of them, so the child-mind in man vacillates from one activity to another. Failure to achieve is the result of scattering the power of the mind over too great an area of endeavor. Man can cultivate no quality more essential to his spiritual well being than that of finishing what he begins. Success can never be achieved in the material world without at least a reasonable development of the power of continuity. In matters pertaining to occultism, the same is true. A person who studies several lines of philosophy may call himself broadminded, but if he carries none of these lines to a successful culmination he is, in reality, "scatter brained." Again and again such a person turns off and tries a new road, when just a few more steps upon the old one would have brought him within sight of achievement.

(3) *The candidate must recognize his debt to society.* If in his zeal to unfold his spiritual nature he neglects those daily labors which have been assigned to him in the material world, he can never hope to attain true spirituality. Each individual born into the physical world has obligations which if not assumed by him must he carried by others. Among the Hindus, for example, the debt which the Brahmin owes to the race that produces him is very keenly felt. This debt is not paid until a son is born to him and he has lavished upon it the parental regard and care which he previously received from his parents.

Woe to those who neglect their fellow creatures to serve their God! In this world it is necessary first to earn the right to leisure time which is essential fair personal improvement. The chief reason why people are always confronted by problems is that they are ever seeking to evade problems. So many say, "Life is just one difficulty after another," when, in reality, it is the same difficulty presenting itself again and again, because it is not mastered. The candidate is urged to face and settle each problem of his life. In this way perplexities are eliminated and more leisure is available for ethical progress. The prosaic duties of daily life are the elements out of which character is built, and those unable to cope with them are as useless in things spiritual as they are in things material.

Occult development is an exceedingly slow process. The results of the time and energy expended are often imperceptible. This brings discouragement; the candidate gives up the struggle, considering the task before him a hopeless one. Discouragement is one of the temptations placed in the way of the candidate by the Mysteries, fear in spiritual matters he who can be discouraged is not worthy of encouragement. It is by means of discouragement that mediocre minds are eliminated. Recognizing the difficulty of preserving mental continuity, the Mysteries demand it of their candidates, for only those who year after year struggle on to the single goal, wandering in darkness but with one-pointedness and perfect faith, are considered worthy to enter the Temple—the House of the Immortals.

(4) *The candidate must realize the importance of motive.* An analysis of motives generally demonstrates them to be basically selfish, regardless of how unselfish they may appear. Only those who assume the study of occultism with the highest and most unselfish motives can hope to succeed in this the supreme science. In the present age nearly every one has ulterior

motives, most of which center around the aggrandizement of the individual not-self, mistaken for the Self. We desire power that we may be recognized as powerful; we desire wisdom that we may be recognized as wise; we gravitate about important people in the hope that we may shine a little with their reflected glory; we seek to be virtuous that one man may say to another, "There goes a godly person!" To the average person it is inconceivable that greatness should not promenade. And yet an analysis of the men and women who have become great—either in spiritual or material affairs—reveals, in the majority of cases, humble, retiring individuals whose greatness is never offensive. Those who study occultism, hoping thereby to improve their material condition, fail utterly. Before power can be safely entrusted to man, he must become supremely indifferent to it. Perfect unselfishness is perfect consecration to the service of the One Universal Self.

Before anyone begins a study of the mystic sciences with the hope that he will add to the dignity of his position or to the weight of his coffers, he should consider for a moment the social, financial, and worldly position of those who during the ages past have been recognized as exponents of occultism and philosophy. Count Cagliostro, languishing for years in prison; Marshal Ney, an exile living under an assumed name; Abbe Villars, murdered for writing his *Romance of the Gnomes*—these are but a few examples demonstrating the rewards which the world holds out to those who try to educate it.

In order to serve more effectively, a few initiates (such as Comte de St. Germain and Francis Bacon) were placed in positions of world power. But with this increased dignity came increased responsibility. The crown of spiritual adeptship is a far heavier one than the crown of material rulership. The use of occultism for the gratification of personal ends constitutes *black magic.*

It is for these reasons that the applicant is asked, "What motive urges you to take up these arts and sciences? Is it your supreme and all ensouling desire to be of unselfish service to humanity?" To these questions some reply, "Gladly will I *die* for truth." To them the answer is, "That is not enough. Will you live for truth?" A few brief moments and the act of martyrdom is consummated; a few seconds of pain and the soul of man is beyond the reach of the executioner. This is a tremendous sacrifice—a glorious death. But the daily living, surrounded by problems and worries, year after year of disappointments this is the supreme test of unselfishness. Until the soul can find perfect joy in giving, perfect companionship in aloneness, perfect sufficiency in the power of truth, perfect abundance in the gratitude of the few and the scorn of the man—until such a state is reached the disciple is not ready to leave the broad road on which the world walks and take the thorn—lined path which leads to conscious immortality.

Years are spent by the Masters testing the hearts of candidates. Those who begin spiritual unfoldment find difficulties of all kinds rising before them. The even tenor of human existence is shattered, temptations of all kinds confront the seeker, and it is only when he rises triumphant above them all that he is usable in the great plan of human progress. In a man of little mind selfishness is a small sin; should that man develop a great mind and control the destinies of thousands, the small sin (if left unmastered) becomes a great menace. The impotent selfishness of ignorance becomes the potent tyranny of power.

Occasionally we find persons who, if not in some way restrained by Nature, would become archdoers of evil. But Nature, Delilah-like, has shorn them of their locks. One such case will suffice to demonstrate the principle: A sardonic iconoclast, with a tongue like a two—edged sword, who ruthlessly—even gleefully—destroyed hope, love, and faith in the hearts of others, was struck with paralysis which, affecting his tongue, made speech a slow and painful process. His heart is still filled with malice; in fact he is more malignant than before, but his power to injure others has been taken from him.

All men are born with many faculties and members paralyzed. Some are filled with malignancy, held in curb only by their inability to vent their spleen. All human beings have latent faculties and powers, but all are not privileged to develop them at this time. Before it would be safe to loosen the tongue of the malignant creature who calls himself a man, it would first be necessary to transmute the bitterness in his heart.

In a similar manner, before it would be advisable to liberate man from the natural paralysis of ignorance, there should be assurance that the newly awakened faculties shall be a blessing to humanity and not a curse. Before the Masters give man the power to loosen his tongue, his heart must be purified so that the power which is given to him shall not frustrate the plan of true spiritual unfoldment. This is the real reason for the periods of probationship. During these periods the mind and heart are cleansed of those things which, if given power of expression, would work evil. When the supreme forces of Nature are placed in the hands of the newly raised initiate, his heart, his mind, and his soul must accept these gifts with divine humility without thought of self, and use them for the greatest good to the greatest number.

(5) *The candidate must shun all kinds of psychism and phenomenalism.* The fundamental purpose of occultism is not to equip a disciple with the power to see auras, elementals, or thought forms. Nor is it concerned with the processes of bringing those who have passed on into communication with bereaved relatives on the material plane. Occultism is, first, an ethical

philosophy; second, an operative science. As the candidate obeys the laws imposed upon him by the Mysteries and as he is faithful in his discharge of the new duties which he is assuming, he gradually and sequentially unfolds the various parts of himself. His faculties become so sensitized that he is able to see at each step of his growth that which is essential for him to see, and sense that which is essential for him to sense. Clairvoyance is an effect and not a cause; it is the result of certain adjustments of the life and a gradual regeneration of the bodily parts and members.

True occult growth is so slow that it is almost imperceptible, the faculties unfolding from within outward like the petals of a flower. To hasten these natural processes beyond a certain point is to endanger the sanity and health of the candidate.

So-called clairvoyance may take many forms. A student may reach a comparatively high degree of *Chelaship* and still be unaware of any extension of sense perception such as is commonly associated with spiritual growth, while a person possessing many psychic powers may be totally unfitted even to enter upon the path of *Chelaship*. One of the surest signs of true occult unfoldment is a peculiar extension of sense perception or of the mental sense of awareness, which might be called "clair~cognizance." The average person would describe this condition as a form of mental clarity or acuteness. Instead of presenting itself through the organs of vision or hearing, occult cognition some times comes in a purely intellectual form, the mind becoming actually aware of occult truths and philosophic verities without any involvement of the lesser senses

An example of this is the student who desires to learn the color vibration of a certain invisible organ or part of the body. The mind instantly replies that it is red, without actually giving any color impression—the information coming more as words imprinted upon the mind than in any other form—yet the mind itself registers no awareness of words spoken either physically or spiritually. Apparently the mind of itself announces the color to be red.

In things pertaining to occult philosophy, this faculty seems to be the particular reward of the teacher. If the lay instructor is actually in contact with the higher worlds he will learn far more while he is teaching than will those to whom he is explaining the subjects under discussion, the "clair-cognizance" revealing spontaneously that which the faculties of the mind under normal conditions could not reason out in months. This is the only so-called psychic faculty the coming of which should not be viewed with a certain amount of apprehension. The premature development of clairvoyance and psychism is a serious impediment to the spiritual growth of the student, who is all too likely to wander astray in the byways of the astral plane and end in the blind alley of transcendentalism.

(6) *The candidate must realize that with the increase of knowledge there is a proportionate increase* of *responsibility.* With the acquirement of knowledge, the student must acquire the sense of discrimination, so that he may use most intelligently the information he has received. Nearly all who take up the study of occultism eventually become teachers of its abstruse sciences. It is proper that they should do this, for as they themselves were instructed they but pay their natural debt by becoming instructors of others.

The lay teacher should realize, however, that he becomes accountable for the use which others make of the knowledge he entrusts to them. He cannot shift this burden on to the Mystery Schools; he must bear it himself. For this reason he must be as wise as the gods if he would save himself from the karmic reactions of the forces which he has enabled others to set in operation.

In occultism the initiate speaks only for himself. Unless actually upon an official errand for the School to which he belongs, he never makes the esoteric Orders in any way responsible for his individual utterances and actions. Unless specifically ordered to do so, the emissaries of the Mysteries speak only for themselves—never for the higher initiates.

Those illumined minds who represent the Schools of the Mysteries in the world need no heralding, nor do they require credentials from the invisible Brotherhood to which they belong. Never do they announce themselves, for their power lies not in their affiliations but in themselves. Why should an initiate tell the world that he is a superman? Unless he demonstrates it by his actions, the world will not accept him as such; and if the exceptional qualities of his intellect prove it, the claim is unnecessary.

All over the world there are hundreds of individuals and institutions claiming to represent the secret Schools of the Ancient Wisdom. Few of these organizations and still fewer of the individuals, can successfully defend their claims in the face of a critical analysis of their principles and policies. Those disciples truly consecrated to the service of the invisible Schools have made it their policy to refrain from even mentioning the august bodies which they so inadequately represent, until that time when the invisible Order no longer could be discredited by their actions. The true disciple would rather die than compromise his Master or the School into which he hopes sometime to be initiated. He can protect the institution only by assuming personal responsibility for all that he says and does. Then his faults disgrace no one but himself.

Only when he has reached the point of complete spiritual illumination does he reveal the source of his knowledge, and then only to a limited few.

One of the laws of occultism is that in order to receive, one must give. Those desirous of greater insight into things spiritual must earn the right to that broader understanding by the intelligent use of that knowledge already possessed. The student-teacher must realize that he is personally responsible for whatever effects his theories and doctrines may have upon the minds and bodies of others. By instruction we actually change the course of others' lives; we direct them into new channels of mental and physical activity; we change the tenor of their existence. If directly or indirectly these changes are not beneficial to them, we who gave them the knowledge become responsible before the gods for the results of our indiscretion.

In a similar manner, those who teach us are responsible for our actions and the use we make of the wisdom they have shared with us. Hence, when the disciple fails, it is the Master who suffers most. Most of all, we are responsible if we place in the hands of those unfitted to receive it that knowledge of Nature's forces which enables one person to injure another. If we are not mentally developed to that point where we can determine beforehand, with a reasonable amount of certainty, the integrity of the person to whom we intend to reveal occult secrets, we are not far enough advanced to possess such secrets ourselves.

In justice to himself, therefore, no one should be in a hurry to go forth serving humanity, lest in his impetuosity he destroy not only others but himself with them. The groundwork should be laid first. When such a one feels that he is equipped to disseminate a message, he should do it reverently, with deep consideration and no little trepidation, saying to himself: "I am responsible from now on for the use and interpretation placed by others upon the words that come out of my mouth. Therefore, I will choose them with care, consider them in the light of my truest and highest intelligence, and send forth with each a prayer that it shall serve only the cause of good. I will not claim to be anything or anyone, but will let my works speak for me, for I am only as great as my works."

If it be the will of the Masters that I should in time reach an exalted position as their messenger, I will then (if they so desire it) be their chosen and authorized mouthpiece. But until the day of that supreme achievement if a man should ask me who I am, I shall answer that I am a voice crying in the wilderness. If he should ask who sent me, I shall answer that my soul sent me. If he should ask by what authority I teach men, I shall answer that I am my own authority. If he should ask what message I bring, I shall answer that I bring no message, but only interpret according to my light that message which is eternally here. And if he should ask, 'What reward have we if we follow you?' I shall answer that the accomplishment of labor is the reward of labor.

(7) *The candidate must maintain a constructive mental attitude.* All thinking people are dissatisfied with existing conditions. They also realize that the universe is ruled by the Law of Cause and Effect, and that in order to improve affairs it is first necessary to establish those remedial and corrective causes the natural result of which will be universal peace and enlightenment.

It is imperative that we accept things as we find them in this world; and instead of complaining or criticizing if they are not in accordance with our desires, let us set about with diligence and intelligence to create newer and better conditions. If his mind be soured or his nature be established in the habit of complaining, the prospective candidate bars himself from the service of the Masters.

Since life is so serious an affair, it has well been said that the sense of humor is a saving grace. We become useless to our fellow creatures if we permit ourselves to he oppressed by the weight of the world's woe. It is a mistake to believe that seriousness can take the place of integrity. There is no substitute for the happy smile or the normal, healthy attitude toward the problems of life. The candidate need not cultivate thoughtless optimism but rather that attitude of mind which sees the hand of God in everything and realizes that all things are working together for the ultimate good of each. The iconoclast is a useful and important member of society, but he never attains the highest state of usefulness because his mind is on a tangent.

Man is much like an apple: some people mellow with age, while others rot; some are deepened and sweetened by experience, while others are hopelessly soured. Those who become soured have failed utterly. They are mentally diseased and incapable of constructive thinking. Sourness is often the result of self~pity, one of the most subtle and terrible forms of egotism. It is egotism that makes people actually believe that they are so important that Nature singles them out to heap infirmities upon them. No one who pities himself has any inherent sense of justice. Without a perfect faith in a natural justice, man cannot attain the heights of either philosophy or religion. Make it one of the fundamental rules of your life that you will never be sorry for yourself. If you become the slave of self-pity, you will soon become a legitimate object of pity on the part of intelligent people.

These seven cardinal requirements therefore constitute the ethical foundation of occultism. Without consecration of the life to the attainment of proficiency in these qualities of character, it is useless to go on—if such a thing were possible. The foundation must come first. Most of the failures in mysticism and philosophy result from neglect of the ethical basis. The superstructure of esotericism must be raised upon the solid rock of virtue and integrity, for without this foundation it inevitably falls.

Man cannot prepare himself for philosophic pursuits in a few weeks or even a few years. He must build slowly and solidly, realizing that one step properly taken is worth many taken haphazard and without direction. When the general self improvement is fairly well advanced, it is then time for the student to prepare himself along certain special lines of endeavor which will peculiarly fit him for occult attainment. This is not the first step but the second, and is not to be taken until the initial groundwork has been *thoroughly* established.

With each advancing step the candidate finds the standards of life more exacting and difficult of attainment, with deviation from these ideals productive of ever increasing sorrow and suffering. The requirements of the law for the initiate are much more strict than for the average individual, for the initiate can possess his transcendent powers only by sacrificing everything else. The would-be disciple of the Ancient Wisdom, after having schooled himself in the seven principles described above, must now turn his attention to the choice of that particular line of endeavor and that particular School of the Mysteries in which he feels he will be most useful. The qualities previously developed by the first ethical training are now tested, for only by their aid can the selection be intelligently made. While the path of accomplishment differs in each School, all the Mystery Schools teach the same fundamental doctrines and ultimately attain the same results.

Let us suppose that you have chosen one of the Eastern Schools. Before you can actually begin your studies, you must familiarize yourself with the particular ethical code which it disseminates. The School will educate you in certain concepts and attitudes which, when incorporated into your life, have a marked effect upon the invisible nature. Only when these effects reach a certain point is it safe for you to begin any special system of so called spiritual development. Although the sevenfold cardinal requirements are applicable to persons in any walk of life (whether religiously or atheistically inclined), the more advanced requirements are concerned directly with the individual needs of the student.

This more advanced code is open to the consideration of all who have conducted themselves worthily according to the primary requirements. But woe to those who, ignorant, selfish, and otherwise unqualified, dabble in any form of occult science without first overcoming the more important faults of the lower nature! The proof of man's sincerity is his willingness to sacrifice, and the occult student must sacrifice his own lower nature if he would enter the Temple of Wisdom.

Again and again, the student of occult philosophy deplores the fact that he cannot discriminate between the true and the false. He reveals his dilemma by saying: "Oh, if I only knew which of the paths of discipleship I ought to take! If I were only sure that this teacher is really qualified to instruct in these subjects! If I could only be certain that this book is the one I should study! But I am afraid to trust my decision on these matters. Won't you please decide for me? Such questions demonstrate beyond all doubt that the mind of the student has not matured to the point where it is capable of discrimination.

Not knowing right from wrong and incapable of dividing the real from the unreal, too many students are seeking advanced spiritual instruction when their ethical education is hopelessly inadequate. If you do not know what you want to do, you are not ready to do anything. You must first develop sufficient ethical perception to be cognizant of what you want to accomplish. The lack of such discrimination is much too common among occultists and is often the unsuspected cause of their inability to attain spiritual unfoldment.

Many students feel that this ethical training, by itself, is a waste of time and that it is far more desirable to become immediately engrossed in arcane traditions. The lack of this mental and moral culture effectually disqualifies the candidate for the steps which follow; the inevitable result is sorrow, suffering, incompetence, and disappointment.

Assuming that you have carefully considered the seven cardinal requirements already described, it is now in order to analyze the more specific factors with which the candidate must familiarize himself.

(1) The first—and most important—is the selection of the person or institution whose instruction will constitute your course of occult procedure. Consider with us for a moment the attitude of the Eastern mystics on this vital subject.

The assistance of a properly qualified teacher is essential to the progress of the student. Just as a plant grows in the light of the sun, warmed and vitalized by its Pranic emanations, so the disciple unfolds, flower-like, nurtured and assisted by the spiritual radiance of his Master.

The aura of a highly evolved adept is also of great assistance to a young student who as yet is unable completely to create certain atmospheres for himself. Gradually the perfect and continued communion between Master and disciple brings them very close together in spiritual understanding. A beautiful friendship is born between the two, which gradually merges into a perfect and impersonal love. The *Guru* (teacher) comes to know the innermost thoughts of his disciples. He tests the student by bringing him into the presence of temptation and encouraging him to be strong. He perceives where the student is weak. He discovers the faults in the nature which inhibit attainment, and by wise counsel aids his "spiritual son" to avoid pitfalls and blind alleys.

While the *Guru* may have many exoteric students, he seldom takes more than twelve at one time into the esoteric phase of his instruction. He realizes that no one can properly direct the studies of too large a number at one time and give each of them the individual help which is so necessary. He realizes that he is the parent of a spiritual infant who is being nurtured in the nature of his disciple, and that this spiritual child needs almost constant attention during the early stages of its growth. By carefully observing these requisites, the Master protects the life and health of his disciples and leads them step by step to the state of accomplishment which they could not reach unaided.

To study for a few weeks or even months with an unknown teacher (even though he may be suspected of having great intelligence), and then to attempt to work out by yourself future exercises and systems of development is the height of madness, for the daily unfoldment resulting from occult exercises requires intelligent supervision by a teacher who is prepared for any and all emergencies. Hence the disciple who undertakes the actual operative processes of spiritual regeneration generally lives (for a time, at least) with his teacher, so that every hour of the day or night the Master is within call. In India, the *chelas* remain with their teachers for an entire lifetime to make certain that each step in their attainment is properly completed and the subsequent work correctly outlined.

Who is qualified to instruct in the operative mysteries of either Eastern or Western occultism? The answer is, *only* an initiate or the disciple of an initiate. An initiate is one whose attainment to a position of spiritual understanding has been in harmony with the laws of attainment. Therefore he must be and is in consistency with the laws which have produced him. Not only this, but he must be of that Ray of the Mysteries which is devoted to teaching. Many great initiates are not in the teaching Ray; therefore never take disciples. Others, again, are so highly advanced that none but initiates are eligible to their instruction, as in the case of the Master J. The laws of attainment demand purity of life and purpose; simplicity of demeanor and appearance; humility of mind and heart; selflessness, kindliness, wisdom, and absolute freedom from the taint of worldliness and commercialism. And on either side of this narrow path which the disciple must walk are the pitfalls of *Dugpa* magic.

We should also bear in mind that there are few, if any, Westerners who are qualified to teach the esoteric principles of Eastern occultism. Many are attempting to do so, but their bungling efforts demonstrate their incompetence. The East deals in subtleties, and occultism is a subtle science, everything depending upon inflections which are totally beyond the average Western intellect.

While Western scholars may learn to understand the general outline of Eastern occultism, even a lifetime in India or Tibet will not qualify them as teachers of Eastern esotericism, unless during their sojourn in the Orient they have actually been initiated into the Eastern Mysteries. Even then there are certain key secrets which the Brahmins, for instance, will not reveal to any person of a race or caste different from their own. For this reason most of the concepts promulgated by Westerners are hopelessly erroneous or, at best, incomplete.

None but the East apparently can understand the East, for it is a world totally different in attitudes and concepts from the one with which we are familiar.

Then, again the Hindus themselves (while far more religious and philosophical as a race than the Western peoples) are not all qualified to teach these abstruse occult sciences. As the average Christian minister is comparatively ignorant concerning mystical Christianity, so a great number of Orientals have little knowledge of the finer points of their faith. While it is true that the percentage of Orientals who understand their religion is much higher than the percentage of Christians who understand Christianity, the mere fact that a person comes from the Orient is no assurance that he is qualified to instruct concerning the secret teachings of his faith. It requires a highly advanced Oriental to adjust his doctrine to the Western world for if presented without certain adjustments it is almost useless.

In choosing an instructor in any line of occult science, then, great care and discrimination must be used and an acid test applied. The point where lack of true understanding is most evident is in the commercial attitude, and if the student will eliminate from his list pseudo occultists with axes to grind, he will escape the majority of the pitfalls.

*(2) The second point is the consideration of the time element.* Time is the primary prerequisite of occult growth. The disciple may expect it to require at least twenty years to attain success in even the first degrees. In the early part of the disciple's training he will probably find it necessary to receive his instruction from someone in the physical world, but as he goes higher and acquires the ability to separate his consciousness from his lower vehicles, he may receive his instruction from teachers and initiates working through the subtle essences of the

invisible worlds.

No layman, either in the East or in the West, is qualified to begin the practice of so-called occult exercises without special preparation covering a period of years. Even in the East, where the mind is concerned with occultism and philosophy from infancy, special preparation is required before even the simplest of the exercises are begun. Even though a student has delved into occultism for years and has attended countless lectures, he is not justified in thinking that he is ready for deep esoteric work. Unless during those years he followed a certain prescribed and systematic course of training, he must begin to do so, and until he has achieved success therein he is not ready for deeper or more complicated forms of culture. Notwithstanding the fact that he considers himself a highly developed person, he must begin at the bottom and pass through his years of probationary work just the same as the disciple who apparently is far less informed. The true occultist realizes that it is not always how long we are at a thing, but how intelligently we pursue our labors that counts; and many who have spent an entire life time have achieved comparatively little.

It is for the *Guru* (and not the *chela*) to decide when the period of probationship is completed, for the teacher is capable of investigating man's invisible spiritual nature, upon which the record of accomplishment is imprinted. The period of time for the first probationship is usually from two to five years. Pythagoras of Crotona demanded five years of self purification before he would even discuss the matter of spiritual unfoldment with a candidate applying for membership in his university.

During these years of preparation the disciple adjusts his entire life to the work to which he looks forward. He becomes permeated with certain spiritual and intellectual attitudes, and thus comes *en rapport* with the holy science. It means that every atom and molecule of his quaternary constitution must be purified and made over. The organism must be unfolded, and every part of the structure must thrill and vibrate in a peculiar manner. What does this mean? It means that the attainment of spiritual power is impossible unless the life, mind, and body are dedicated entirely to that labor. It also means that so much depends upon the teacher into whose hands the student places himself that it is, in reality, a matter of life and death.

(3) *The third point for the candidate to realize is the necessity of remaining silent concerning any esoteric secrets which may be revealed to him.* He may discuss the theoretical part of occultism with any whom he feels deserving of such information, but the operative secrets he must reveal to no one. They are given to him as Master to disciple, and are for him alone. The curse of the gods is upon the head of the man who reveals the hiding place of his Lord for thirty pieces of silver.

The Christ in you is the secret and powerful spiritual nature—the miracle worker, the divine, invisible man. The one who reveals the nature and power of this secret Lord betrays his divine Master (the spiritual nature) and turns its power over to the hands of the mob (his own lower animal nature). At the hands of the mob, the Christ (the secret power) is crowned with a wreath of thorns and taunted as a king. He is given the kingdom of death to rule and is scourged by the soldiers. In the hands of the mob nature in man, the secret and divine power, which has thus been betrayed, is crowned with sorrow; the divine science is prostituted that ignorant mortals may by the aid of spiritual powers secure material prosperity, marital happiness, or improve lagging business conditions.

Approach with the utmost care, therefore, the subject of

occult exercises. Remember that the esoteric secrets of occultism are designed for the use of only that illumined few who, having first consecrated their lives to the unfoldment of the spiritual powers latent within them, have reached a point after many years where they are qualified to assume the responsibility of liberating their spiritual natures from the bondage of matter. For the layman—ethically unprepared and wholly ignorant concerning the operation of occult currents and forces—to dabble with any form of occult exercises is almost certain to result disastrously.

(4) The candidate must realize the great danger of becoming involved in black magic. The line of demarcation between black and white magic is so fine that even those highly advanced must exercise eternal watchfulness in order to avoid involvements in *Dugpa* sorcery. To a great degree, the difference between black and white magic lies in the motive. An impersonal and unselfish attitude is the surest protection against black magic, but many other things (especially self- control) are necessary to insure that the candidate shall escape the dangers of sorcery. Both the white magician and the black magician use identical forces. The former, however, grows through his constructive use of the divine sciences, whereas the latter slowly but inevitably destroys himself by their perversion.

The attainment of transcendental powers must be either through the regeneration and scientific reconstruction of the body—the gradual liberation of the consciousness enmeshed within the form—or else through sorcery, black magic, and necromancy. Woe to him who believes even for a moment that he can tamper with black magic and survive! Both the East and West are filled with *Dugpas*—black magicians, who by the perversion of occult forces have become temporarily manipulators of cosmic energy. Gradually, but inevitably, these

*Dugpas* are drawn into the maelstrom of their own evil and perish. The great danger which confronts haphazard students is that they may develop spiritual forces within their bodies to a degree where they can be used by the *Dugpas* for one purpose or another before they have developed the strength and enlightenment to use these forces to any good end. Thus many really good people become unconscious doers of evil because they are not sufficiently intelligent to understand the right application of the forces they have awakened within themselves.

(5) *The candidate must realize that the application of commercial terms to occult values is a direct prostitution of this most sacred of all sciences.* While a teacher of philosophy (like a professor of botany or mathematics) may be, and should be, remunerated for his efforts (which remuneration may be accepted to a moderate degree without prostituting his science), the operative secrets of occultism must never be involved in any form of commercialism. They have no commercial value. To attempt the buying or selling of them is one of the most heinous of sins.

By *operative secrets* we mean that knowledge which will assist the individual to personally unfold by secret, but scientific, processes the latent forces or faculties of his own nature. These must not, shall not, and can not be bought or sold.

When a man is decorated by a government for a deed of valor, he does not have to buy the medal that is pinned on his breast. The same rule applies with respect to the secret doctrines which is revealed to man as the reward for spiritual, moral, and intellectual valor. When the disciple is ready, it is an inconceivable and unpardonable sin to deny him that which is his by right of merit. To sell the secrets of the invisible world to one unworthy to know them and incapable of earning them, is sacrilege; to try to sell them to one who has already earned that wisdom by virtue of the superior qualities of his own nature is also a sacrilege.

To place the great secrets of occultism in writing is dangerous and brings a heavy karmic debt down upon the head of the one so foolish as to do it; and to sell a document containing such secrets compounds his karmic obligations. When revealed to the public, all material dealing with operative occultism must be veiled then it seems desirable to reveal the theory behind these processes, certain keys must always be omitted, so that a careless reader may not be able to hurt himself by experimenting with the information thus gained. These facts are well known to those entrusted with esoteric information, and any who break these rules demonstrate their total unfitness to instruct students in the mysteries of the occult sciences.

*(6) The candidate must beware of unbalance.* Equilibrium can be safeguarded by continual emphasis of the ideal of symmetry. The student should always bear in mind that one virtue is not sufficient to make a saint, no matter how excellent that one virtue may be. Man must grow symmetrically—his heart, his mind, and his body must coordinate and complement each other. He must achieve the condition of mental, spiritual, and physical equilibrium. If the mind is over developed, the scientist results; if the heart dominates, the religious fanatic and emotionalist is produced; if the physical nature controls, the materialist is the inevitable product. It is only when all three of these parts unite in the glorification of the divine nature that the composite unit—the spiritual philosopher—becomes a reality.

The most common occult exercises taught to the general public today are various forms of concentration and breathing. Many of these exercises are hopelessly incorrect. Both concentration and breathing (when properly understood) have their place, for both profoundly influence the entire constitution of man. But neither of these alone nor both together will produce any permanent or satisfactory results, unless at the same time the nature possesses certain other virtuous qualities and has adjusted itself to the general plan of spiritual unfoldment. You may use a perfectly correct form of Yoga breathing, but if your body is impure you will never attain any but harmful results.

You may sacrifice all to your gods and be a vegetarian for an entire lifetime, and yet practically nullify the good resulting from these practices by failure to control an obstinate temper which you have tolerated in spite of efforts you have made to overcome other faults. The possible value of any concentrative exercise which you may attempt will be destroyed by an un-eradicated streak of selfishness; an unconquered egotism will continually prevent the consummation of a lifetime of endeavor. If you dislike but one person, you can never attain upon the path of white magic. Any occult development which may be made without conquering these qualities within the nature lays the student open to the perils of *Dugpa* sorcery and black magic.

It is because of the necessity of controlling and transmuting all of the lower qualities of the nature that the years of probationship are so essential. During this period of battle with self, the sincere student gets hold of the threads of his life and begins to make the adjustments necessary before the actual spiritual work can begin. It is not by destroying the lower nature that man becomes virtuous; it is by the transmutation and regeneration of every base quality and attitude that he achieves divinity. This gradual process of self-conquest ultimately brings the disciple to the state of complete self control. From that point attainment is not so difficult, for having controlled self, he is the master of the universe.

All occultists know that true spirituality is not to be gained through either extremes or excesses. Those who try to become ascetics by retiring from the world and rejecting the problems of life, those who fast, those who neglect the problem of daily existence—such cannot achieve, for in the last analysis, only that which is natural and in harmony with common sense can produce permanent benefit. It is the failure to observe these requisites that has caused so much misunderstanding with respect to occultism today. People desire to unfold clairvoyant powers and enter a Nirvana of happiness, peace, and selfish enjoyment. They believe that occultism will vicariously solve their problems. All this is wrong, for no one can attain occultism who has not first given up the desire for earthly happiness and proved his courage and ability to master the problems which beset him in this mortal sphere.

(7) The candidate must next consider the esoteric interpretation of the so called material arts and sciences. Astronomy, mathematics, music, rhetoric, geometry, grammar, and logic are often called the seven liberal arts and sciences. There are, in reality, forty-nine great arts and sciences. An extract from occult anatomy will show how esoteric science differs from material—or exoteric—science.

Turn to the painting of the seven spinal *chakras*. In the picture the general form of the *chakras* has been carefully preserved, special emphasis being placed upon the correct number of petals. In the secret teachings, to each of these petals is assigned a letter of the Sanskrit alphabet. The human figure has been made semi-transparent, as it might appear to one actually gazing upon a Yogi in meditation. The Yogi is apparently suspended in the air, for the power of sight which

**THE SEVEN SPINAL CHAKRAS**

This painting of the Chakras is based upon a number of native drawings brought from India by Mr. Hall in 1924. In the Orient, diagrams of the Chakras are comparatively common, but several symbols not generally included have been added, which make the painting more complete. The most important additions consist of (1) the interlaced triangles behind the figure, the body of the Yogi himself forming the upright triangle; (2) the beam of golden light rising from the Brahmarandra or Gate of Brahma, in the crown of the head; and (3) the Sahasrara, or Thousand-Petaled Lotus, in the upper part of the brain, which is generally pictured as an inverted lotus-like cap but is here shown as a great flower-like sunburst, with a white center and concentric rings of petals.

would enable one to see the *chakras* would take no cognizance of the physical earth upon which he is sitting. The plate is, of course, diagrammatic and must not be considered too literally.

Study carefully the flower-like centers upon the spinal column of the Yogi. Through the center of the seven flowers passes the tube *Sushumna,* which corresponds to the sixth ventricle of science, a tiny tube passing through the center of the spinal cord.

On the left side of *Sushumna* is another tube called *Ida*, and on the right side a third called *Pingala.* These are the poles of the central tube—the sharp and flat of *Sushumna* itself. These two tubes are profoundly influenced by the nostrils on their respective sides. The *Ida* and *Pingala* cross at the base of the skull and both rise out of the four-petaled lotus at the base of the spine. The *Ida, Sushumna,* and *Pingala* together are the chief of the *Nadis*, and of these three the *Sushumna* is the most important. In the ordinary individual the tube of the *Sushumna* is closed, but by Yoga it is opened so that there is a direct connection between the sacral plexus at the base of the spine and the pineal gland in the head.

According to Hindu allegory, *Kundalini*—the goddess of the serpent fire—descends into man through the umbilical cord at the navel, but when the umbilical cord is cut, this serpentine power coils itself in the sacral plexus, where it rests upon the triangular bone at the end of the sacrum. This triangular bone is shown as an inverted triangle in the *Muladhara,* the four-petaled-lotus-blossom at the base of the spine. Here *Kundalini* remains coiled until through occult exercises she is caused to rise through *Sushumna* into the brain, where she awakens the activity of the third eye—the pineal gland. This third eye is the link connecting man with the spiritual world or, to be more correct, with the higher spiritual nature of himself.

The *anthropos,* or *overman,* which never descends into incarnation, was called by the Greeks the *Cyclops*—the giant who had but one eye, which eye was the pineal gland, by means of which the higher ego was capable of seeing downward into the human nature and the human ego was capable of seeing upward into *Buddhi,* or the *overman. Kundalini* is more or less excited into rising as the result of the ascending essences in *Ida* and *Pingala.*

Here we have the *caduceus* of Hermes. The two serpents coiled around the staff are *Ida* and *Pingala* the central staff is *Sushumna,* the bulb at the upper end of the rod is Sahasrara, and the wings are Ajna—the two-petaled-lotus above the bridge of the nose. There is some dispute among Eastern occultists as to whether the pineal gland is actually the thousand petaled lotus. Some affirm that it is, others that it is not but that a higher center in the brain is actually the *Sahasrara.*

Let us now consider the centers from the lower upward. That division or step of Yoga called *Pranayama* is devoted to awakening *Kundalini* from her coils and causing her to rise upward through the *chakras.* As she contacts these in turn they result in an extension of consciousness. Each of the five lower centers distributes one of the five forms of *Prana,* or the broken up energy of the sun. Each of the seven *chakras* also has a corresponding *tattva,* or breath—a motion or condition of spiritual air. Beginning at the bottom of the spine and working upward, the centers are as follows:

First, *Muladhara.* This has four petals and an inverted triangle in the center. The *tattvic* power of smell is associated with this *chakra.* It is probably correlated with the Church of Ephesus mentioned in the Book of Revelation, and corresponds to the sacral ganglion of modern science.

Second, *Svadhishthana.* This is the second from the bottom and contains six petals, with a crescent in the center. Its *tattvic* correspondent governs the sense of taste. It probably corresponds to the Church of Pergamos and is the prostatic plexus of modern science.

Third, *Manipura.* This is the third *chakra* from the bottom, containing the red triangle. It has ten petals and is associated with the epigastric plexus and the navel. Of the seven churches it is probably Smyrna and is associated with the *tattva of sight.*

Fourth, *Anahata.* This is the fourth from the bottom and its symbol is two interlaced triangles. This *chakra* has twelve petals and is associated with what was commonly called today the cardiac plexus. It is probably the Church of Thyatira and its *tattvic* power is the sense of touch.

Fifth, *Vishuddha.* This is the fifth *chakra* from the bottom and consists of a white circle surrounded by sixteen petals. It is known to modern science as the pharyngeal plexus. Its *tattvic* correspondent gives the sense of hearing and it is probably related to the Church of Sardis.

Sixth, *Ajna.* This is the cavernous plexus of the brain and is the sixth from the bottom. The lotus consists of two petals caused by the fanning out of spiritual rays, one to either side. It is probably related to the Church of Philadelphia and its *tattvic* power is to give the quality of thought.

Seventh, *Sahasrara.* This is the thousand-petaled lotus, the highest of the sacred seven. Its *tattvic* power is purely spiritual. It is probably related to the Church of Laodicea and corresponds either with the pineal gland or an unknown center directly above it. When *Kundalini* reaches this point, divine consciousness is attained.

The passage of *Kundalini* upward towards *Sahasrara* is

marked by a gentle warmth. As it rises the lower part of the body becomes cold, until only the head remains warm. The condition is also accompanied by other phenomena. Woe to the unhappy mortal who raises *Kundalini* prematurely to the brain! The sting of the fiery serpent is most deadly, as those well know who have seen the results of her premature raising. She will burn her way to the brain and destroy the reasoning qualities of the mind.

Such, in brief, is the story of the *chakras* and that science called Yoga—the art of developing and controlling them. The story of these centers is clearly set forth in the Book of Revelation, where the seven seals, the seven trumpets, the seven vials, and the seven voices all refer to the spinal centers and the various mysteries concerning them.

The warning cannot be too strongly emphasized that, while the study of the theory of Yoga will acquaint you with many of the mysteries of Nature and of your own constitution, the practice of it should be limited to such as have united themselves with those schools of Eastern philosophy, of which it is the esoteric work. It is well that all should know the theory, but woe to the foolish mortal who attempts the practice without proper instruction and guidance!

The system of training through which disciples must pass in order to prepare themselves for the highest honors of occultism is rigorous. Take, for example, the eight steps which the Yogi is expected to climb to union with his Divine Self. While these processes differ in each of the Schools, they are equally severe and exacting in all; for it is only after the neophyte has shown his ability to master and directionalize every force in his organism that he is given the secret keys by means of which he can control the destiny of creation.

The eight steps of the Yogi School are: *Yama, Niyama,*

*Asana, Pranayama, Pratyahara, Dharana, Dhyana,* and *Samadhi.* What does each stage imply? What qualities must the disciple unfold in order to reach the final stage of perfect spiritual union with the Supreme Self? These are questions which we shall try to answer.

The first step is *Yama.* Under the heading of *Yama,* an exceedingly strict control of the mental nature begins, for the disciple is placing his foot upon the first step which leads to Self. Here he must cease destructive activities forever. He must no longer kill either the body, the hope, or the faith of any living creature. He must become absolutely truthful. His words must be carefully thought out before they are spoken. In spite of his truthfulness, he must never hurt.

Unquestionable honesty must be cultivated. He must not even desire after a thing which is not his own; and he must also give up the sense of possession over that which is his own, realizing that it is only loaned to him that he may use it for the glorification of God. He must cease receiving gifts of any kind. The only thing which he is permitted to receive is sufficient food for his existence and sufficient clothing to cover his body. (This last is not literally practical in the Western world.)

He must gradually cultivate a beauty within his own soul so that he radiates peace, tranquility, harmony, and strong yet merciful sympathy. He must live to do good, serving all things and loving all things. He must have no enmity, but must love his enemies as he loves his friends, and both of these he must love impersonally.

Only when he has accomplished this has he actually achieved the first step in his long path toward the liberation of Self. It is only when we have achieved this perfect peace within ourselves that we are ready to go on; yet how many

American students are trying to concentrate and develop spiritual powers who have not even begun the conquest of their lower natures or the purification of their bodies! This is one of the chief contributory causes behind the tragedies of modern occultism.

The second step is *Niyama*. This stage is even more difficult than the first, for it demands perfect self-control. It also requires the perfect conservation of energy. Wasteful expenditures of life energies must cease. Nothing shall be wasted; the tongue shall be held in restraint to speak only when speech is necessary; the energies of all parts of the body shall be conserved and used only to accomplish that which is essential. Then must come cleanliness of mind, soul, and body for unless all parts are clean in their structure and expression, spirituality cannot be attained.

There must come the development of the sense of peace—the realization that all things are as they should be; that all activity is united to the attainment of good; that the Supreme One is actually controlling His world. In this stage the disciple reads the books of wisdom; familiarizes himself with the secret Scriptures, and ponders and meditates upon the symbols and allegories. To consummate this stage, he surrenders himself and all that he is to God, living only to serve God, existing only to fulfill the dictates of God, offering his hands and his feet, his heart and his mind to God, and claiming nothing for himself. He must withhold nothing. Regardless of his own likes and dislikes, he must offer himself to the Supreme One without reservation or hesitation. Whatever God wills to be done, he will do it; at all times of the day or night he is at the command of the Father. When he has achieved this perfect condition of willingness to be that which God would will him to be, the disciple is then ready to begin the study of body postures—an art which serves many purposes.

The third step is *Asana.* The purpose of this step is to gain control over the muscles and members of the physical body. It is one of the secret sciences, and consists of a series of body postures, the assuming of which causes various muscles and nerves to come into play which otherwise are not used. Its consummation is the ability of the mind to control the function of every organ and part of the human body, so that when the mind so wills, the heart will stop beating and the individual still live. This complete bodily control has a considerable influence upon the length of life, and according to the Hindus, will considerably lengthen the span of human existence.

A careful consideration of these stages will reveal the fact that they are all devoted to the problem of mastering the not-self and bringing the tangible nature under the control of the intangible spiritual man. When this stage has been successfully passed, the candidate comes to the next step, which is the control of the solar force within the body.

*The fourth step is called Pranayama.* This involves to a certain degree the science of breathing. *Prana* is the life power from the sun. The flow of this force can be controlled by the mind and, to a certain degree, by the breath. There is a certain individuality in breathing. This individuality can be affected by timing the breath and is somewhat governed by the nostril used in inhaling and exhaling.

*Pranayama* is closely related to the science of the *chakras,* for by means of its exercises the goddess *Kundalini* is caused to rise through the spinal canal. It also has to do with the purifying of the nerves, for the *Pranic* energy flows through the nerve canals. This is a hazardous procedure, however, for the average Occidental, and he is warned to leave it entirely alone unless he has already advanced through many stages of spiritual growth.

It is far better and wiser not to discuss the exact method by means of which this breath force is directed.

The fifth step is *Pratyahara*. At this point the disciple begins one of the most difficult of all occult processes the control of the mind. Few people realize how wild and erring their minds are. The mind wanders ever from one thing to another. Control seems almost impossible, for the very element with which it must be controlled is the element which is wandering.

*Pratyahara* may be termed the process of separating the mind from the illusions of the senses and turning it more and more upon the contemplation of Reality. The mind must be controlled: it must think only when it is told to think and as it is told to think; it must be directionalized by the will of the individual. When man is master of his thoughts and feelings, when he is in perfect possession of his mind, he has accomplished the fifth step. Today the average person cannot think clearly because interest sways his judgment. He thinks in favor of the things he loves and against the things he hates; he blames some people and exonerates others, when both are guilty of similar offenses. This is because the mind is a servant of the senses and is incapable of free and unprejudiced thought.

To the correction of this the mind and the senses are gradually separated, so that the desires, lusts, greeds, and passions are no longer capable of turning the mind from the contemplation of things as they are. When this has been accomplished, the disciple is then ready for the next step.

The sixth step is *Dharana*. The mind, having been controlled, is now directionalized. It is turned to this point or to that and held there unwaveringly. In order to be most useful to man, the mind must be capable of pointing. It must reach such a condition that, like a single beam of light, it can be turned in any direction and held there for any desired length of time. When placed in a certain position, the mind remains there until the will of the operator moves it.

When the stage of *Dharana* is achieved, the center of intelligence seemingly can be moved so that it is centered in almost any part of the body. The sense of feeling can be restricted to any given area. By this means the mind also can be forced to turn inward and see the internal parts of the body. It profoundly influences whatever point to which it is directed, because it is so finely pointed that its shaft is almost solid enough to affect the physical organs. When all thought can be enclosed and limited to certain areas at will, it is called the accomplishment of *Dharana*.

The seventh step is *Dhyana*. This is a continuation of the previous step and is the natural outcome of it. When the mind has become capable of pointing itself to any part of the human structure and of being held there continuously, a condition of contemplation results. In this way, an understanding of the invisible causal nature of the object contemplated is achieved; or as one Eastern mystic says, "The mind begins to flow towards the point established." Gradually everything else ceases to exist except the point, and the mind, absorbing its lower illusionary nature, draws near to a perfect knowledge and conscious of itself.

The eighth and final step is *Samadhi*. It is attained when the mind is capable of ascending higher by its pointing or focalizing than the sense of I. The individual lives, he is conscious, and he thinks; but he is above the sense of *I*. He is temporarily universalized, and when he returns to his normal state of consciousness he brings back with him an overwhelming sense of the relationship of things which he never before possessed.

*Samadhi* is brought on by a tremendous exertion of will

power, in which the mind turns its focal ray to contemplate something greater even than itself. Thinking of this tremendous thing, it is temporarily part of the thing of which it thinks, and dwells in limitless Space and limitless Mind. The mind later drawing itself downward from *Samadhi* enters the restricted area of human intelligence to experience a sense of oppression as a person might feel if he were ushered into a small, ill-ventilated, poorly lighted room.

## A SYNTHETIC EMBLEMATIC CROSS

The theme of this painting is a symbolic cross designed by Mr. Hall in the early summer of 1923. The cross represents a composite of the emblems and figures of the various Mystery Schools gathered to form one harmonious pattern, thus signifying the unification of all religious and philosophic doctrines into one perfect and beautiful unit—a condition which must first come to peas before the ideals of Universal Brotherhood can be realized. The original design has not been altered in any way, but in the oil painting two additions have been made. The first addition is the radiating spectrum behind the cross and the second is the chain of twelve globes, the latter signifying the zodiacal constellations in their appropriate colors. Soon after the design wee completed, the cross was reproduced in diamonds, platinum, gold and enamel, and presented to Mr. Hall by his Los Angeles congregation.

## A Synthetic Emblematic Cross

The cross is the most universal of all religious symbols. Examples of crosses are to be found in the sculpture of nearly all ancient peoples. A cross was hung about the necks of the initiates of the Eleusinian Mysteries of Greece. It was painted upon the foreheads of candidates passing through the pyramid Mysteries of Central America, and is a symbol for God among the North American Indians.

It is a curious fact that the cross, or X, has been so often associated with the power of the decimal system, being the Roman numerical symbol for 10. A similarly shaped hieroglyph is used by both the Japanese and Chinese for the number 10. Crosses have been discovered in the temples of the Brahmins.

One of the most remarkable is an emblem of cruciform pattern found in the Brahmin temples carved out of rock on the Island of Elephanta in the harbor of Bombay.

When the Spaniards arrived in Central America, they discovered the Maya Indians worshipping crosses. At least one of these Maya crosses found its way into a Christian cathedral and now stands unchanged above the high altar.

The Egyptian cross of life—the *crux ansata*--was often referred to as the key to the Mysteries. Many of the gods and goddesses of the Egyptian pantheon are shown carrying the *crux ansata* in their hands, and it was not uncommon to bury these emblems with the dead. Several Egyptian carvings show blessings in the form of crosses issuing from the mouths of the gods, and when the Pharaoh pardoned his enemies the words of pardon are similarly shown.

In its wanderings, the *crux ansata* reached the Easter Islands, far off the coast of South America. There is now an Easter Island figure in the British Museum, brought there many years ago by a sailing ship, which shows the Egyptian cross of life clearly and unmistakably carved upon the reverse side of the statue.

There is also a radiating spectrum, the colors of which symbolize the rates of vibration through which manifest the seven creative Spirits. The spectrum is also a suitable emblem for the auric bodies radiating from the purified and regenerated soul. From each of the twelve globes pours a stream of force. These represent the celestial zodiac—twelve divine, eternal lights, each symbolized by a suitable color. The signs begin with the upper left globe (which is red) and is denominated Aries; they continue from left to right throughout the zodiac. The second globe is red-orange and is called Taurus; the third—orange—is Gemini; and so on around the entire circle.

The cross, then, is a synthetic emblem, combining the emblems of the Mystery Schools as these symbols are united in the nature of man. All of the symbols of the Mystery Schools exist within man and are related to certain centers of his consciousness. Thus, this cross is a macrocosmic and microcosmic figure, setting forth the mystery of human regeneration as that mystery is concealed within the seven lesser and five greater Schools of Divine Wisdom.

The custom of crucifying candidates at the time of initiation into the Mysteries is very old. The Greeks and Persians included symbolic crucifixions in the initiatory rituals of their Mysteries. Candidates were sometimes laid upon cross~shaped altars, at other times they were actually bound to crosses of wood or stone.

The Scandinavian Drottarsused crosses in their rituals, and the *fylfot* cross (more commonly known as the swastika) is a symbol sacred to the Chinese, the Hindus, the Scandinavians, and the American Indians. It is also called the hammer of Thor. It is a spinning cross and is used by the Orientals to symbolize the spinning vortices of force in the spinal chakras.

The Druids worshiped their God, *Hu*, under the form of an oak tree, whose top was cut off some feet above the ground and fastened crosswise to the top of the vertical trunk. The Persians also revered the cross and used it to symbolize Ahura Mazda, their god of light and truth.

Since the cross was an object of universal adoration, it is difficult to find a more fitting basis for a synthetic symbol. It is incorrect to look upon the cross as an exclusive Christian symbol or limited in any way to Christianity. Even the most bigoted investigator must accept the universality of the cross—the supreme symbol of life, regeneration, forgiveness, and resurrection among all peoples of the pagan and Christian worlds.

Many early writers did not associate Christ with the cross. The story of His crucifixion was apparently originated sometime after His death. Christians revere this emblem as a constant reminder of the supreme sacrifice of their leader, while the pagans view it as emblematic of the processes in Nature by means of which growth and unfoldment are continued through the periods of cosmic manifestation. Among the Buddhists and Brahmins, the cross is an emblem of life, light, and truth, and not connected with the Passion of Jesus Christ. It is revered as typical of the supreme and eternal sacrifice of the spiritual forces of Nature, so perverted and destroyed by the sins of the flesh, which must be regenerated and transmuted before the candidate is eligible for acceptance into the fraternity of the immortals.

In our design the cross is white, the color of purity. The four arms of the cross are commonly associated with the four elements, from which the lower bodies of all living things are formed. Man has a mental body, an astral body, a vital body, and a physical body. In the midst of these dwells his spiritual nature, crucified in the form of a flower upon substantial substances.

The cross with its four symbolic beasts—the famous Cherubim of Ezekiel and Revelation—is symbolic of the mind, the heart, the vitality, and the physical nature. Physical substance itself is divided into four major divisions or elements, commonly called earth, water, fire, and air, and known to science as carbon, hydrogen, nitrogen, and oxygen. These four are the basis of all material form and are appropriately symbolized by the cross. The cross is the symbol of the tangible, visible constitution of the human being.

By stretching out his arms, man causes his body to assume the shape of a cross. Thus, the white cross signifies the purified body of the candidate cleansed and prepared to enter the temple of the Mysteries. The Egyptian priests wore only linen robes when entering the temples of their gods. While they often protected their bodies from the excesses of temperature by enveloping themselves in furs, it was considered necessary to leave the skins of animals outside the temple; for nothing pertaining to the animal is worthy to enter the house of God. By the animal is understood, of course, man's animal nature—the irrational part of himself—for nothing but the rational part is capable of knowing or worshipping the gods.

The cross may be black to symbolize impurity, or white to symbolize purity. It may be silver to symbolize fecundity, or gold as emblematic of spiritual virility. In every case it typifies the condition of man's nature. When of base metal, it represents the unregenerate man; when of wood, the sufferer; when of stone, the intellectually and spiritually impotent. In short, the cross is the symbol of the expression of the objective, visible constitution of man; and the substances of which it is composed signify the spiritual status of the objective nature.

Behind our symbolic cross is a zodiac surrounding a series of forty-nine emanating lines (not shown in the plate). The lines represent the forty nine fires or spiritual centers which are objectified in both the Macrocosm and the Microcosm. The zodiac represents the twelve Holy Animals.

Pythagoras taught a peculiar doctrine of transmigration, claiming that the souls of men took upon themselves the bodies of animals. What he really meant was that the souls of mankind, coming into creation through the zodiacal band, took upon themselves the forms of the constellations; for all forms of cosmic life come into manifestation through one of the constellations and are therefore said to assume the forms of beasts.

Crucified upon the cross is the seven-rayed Logos—the one spiritual Creator, manifested through His seven Logi or Planetary Lords, each of which is represented by a point of the star. The colors upon the points are somewhat arbitrary, but there is a reason why they are in the peculiar order shown. Although Mercury is usually symbolized as yellow, here it is violet, because the latter color is composed of blue (the spiritual nature) and red (the animal nature); the mind (Mercury) is the point of blending between them.

The triangles at the extremities of the cross signify the elements, and the diamonds the spiritual essences manifesting through the elements. The twelve knobs on the arms of the cross are the twelve Schools of the Mysteries and the twelve disciples who ate the last supper with their Lord. The knobs are also the twelve Initiates constituting the Great White Lodge—the twelve Immortal Mortals who control the destiny of the world. In the midst of the cross is a fifth diamond (a fifth element) the sacred element of the ancients.

The center of the cross symbolizes the heart—the seat of the divine spiritual nature in man. Outside the diamond is a rose enclosed within the cup of a ten-petaled lotus, thus combining the Rosicrucian and Buddhist Mysteries. The diamond in the midst of the cross is the Philosopher's Stone—the human soul, produced through a transmutation and regeneration of the four elements which, tinctured with the spiritual soul power, are transmuted from base metals into gold.